# A Kid's Guide to

# COLLECTING
# COINS

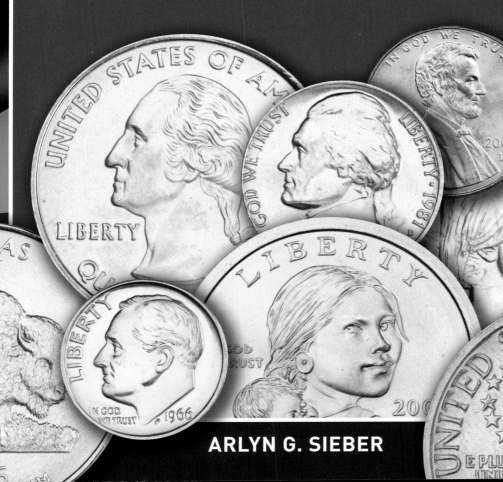

## ARLYN G. SIEBER

Published by

Krause Publications, a division of F+W Media, Inc.
700 East State Street • Iola, WI 54990-0001
715-445-2214 • 888-457-2873

To order books or other products call toll-free 1-800-258-0929
or visit us online at www.shopnumismaster.com

ISBN-13: 978-1-4402-2390-7
ISBN-10: 1-4402-2390-4

Designed by Sharon Bartsch
Edited by Caitlin Spaulding

Printed in China

# TABLE OF CONTENTS

# CHAPTER

## 1

# BE PROUD.
# BE A COLLECTOR.

Did you ever look for something for a while and then find it? Maybe it was a new release of a video game, or a hot new style of athletic shoes, or a hot new style of jeans.

Do you remember how you felt when you finally found that item in the store? Were you excited? Were you anxious to buy it? Did you want to own it right away? If you were lucky enough to get it right away, were you thrilled to finally own it? Were you excited to tell your friends?

Coin collectors know that feeling all the time. They look for coins that will fill spots in their collection, and it's exciting when they find them.

When you found that hot new video game or pair of shoes or pair of jeans, you may not have had the $50 or more it cost to buy them. And maybe your parents weren't in the mood to buy them for you that day. Maybe you had to wait for your birthday or a holiday to get them. Maybe you never got them.

But when you collect coins from pocket change, you can add to your collection for as little as 25 cents or 5 cents or even 1 cent. And you can enjoy a certain pride when you find a coin that fills a certain spot in a coin folder. And that pride increases as you fill other spots in the folder, and it continues every time you open that folder and view your progress toward a complete collection. It also continues when you show off your collection to family and friends.

Over the years, millions of coin collectors started this way. They watched for coins in their own pocket change or their mom's and dad's pocket change, and the ones that filled spots in a collection were popped into a coin folder. Many of today's older collectors remember those days fondly, because it started them on a hobby that they have enjoyed ever since.

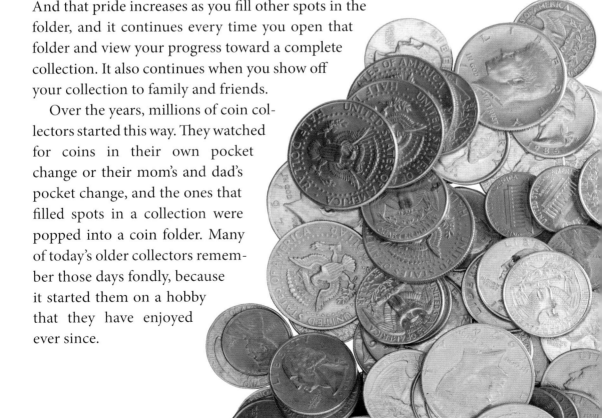

# STILL NEED MORE REASONS TO COLLECT COINS? WELL, HERE YOU GO.

### Anybody can do it

It doesn't matter how fast you can run. It doesn't matter what subjects you're good at in school. It doesn't matter how popular you are. It doesn't matter how old you are, and it doesn't matter whether you're a boy or a girl.

Coin collecting is for everybody. People from all walks of life collect coins.

### It's cheap

Sure, experienced collectors can spend hundreds or even thousands of dollars on an old coin. But you don't have to be rich to collect coins.

It can cost only 1 cent to add a coin found in pocket change to a collection of Lincoln cents.

And don't think those experienced collectors who spend thousands of dollars on an old coin will look down on you for it. That's how they started when they were kids.

### You'll learn stuff without even trying

In what year was President Abraham Lincoln born? Ask any older coin collector that question and he or she can quickly give you the answer – 1809.

Why? Because they know that the Lincoln cent was first produced in 1909 to mark the 100th anniversary of Lincoln's birth. They also know that the Lincoln Memorial design on the cent's reverse (or tails side) was first produced in 1959 to

Abraham Lincoln with his youngest son, Tad.

Obverse and reverse of 1909-S VDB Lincoln cent.

mark the 150th anniversary of Lincoln's birth.

They also know that several special 1 cent coins were produced in 2009 to mark the 200th anniversary of Lincoln's birth.

Learning stuff like this just comes with the hobby. No extra effort is needed.

## It can make homework easier

You'll still have to do your homework, but coin collecting can help you remember facts about U.S. history and other subjects.

Do you need a project for a class at school? Your coin collection might be able to help there, too. Coins can be part of history, civics, math, and other subjects.

## Coins last forever

Those hot new athletic shoes or jeans will wear out or go out of style, but coins in a collecting folder keep pretty much forever. There is little that can harm them.

Sometimes collectors spend time on other things for a while, but their coins are always waiting for them when they return. Many older collectors still have the coins they first collected as kids.

## It's easy

There are just a few simple things you need to know to start collecting coins. And you can learn those things in this book.

There are a lot of other things you can learn about coins and collecting, but you don't need to know them all to start. As you continue to collect, you'll learn more, and your collecting knowledge will grow.

### There's never been a better time to start

The United States has issued many collectible coins in recent years. Among the best known are the State quarters and now quarters honoring the country's national parks and other national sites.

These collectible coins can be found in pocket change. You just need to know what to look for, and this book will tell you that. This book will also give you some special tips to help you find these coins.

### The value of coin collecting

Will a State quarter you find in pocket change ever be worth more than 25 cents? Hmmm. Probably not. But that's not why many people collect coins.

People like to collect coins because they enjoy their designs, they enjoy learning about the people and places shown on coins, they enjoy finding a coin that fills a spot in their folder, and they enjoy looking at their collections or a collection in progress.

Yes, it's true: some collectors have purchased old coins, saw them increase in value over time, and then sold them for a lot of money. But these collectors all had one thing in common: They truly enjoyed the coins they owned, and they truly enjoyed learning about them.

And chances are, these people started collecting when they were kids by searching pocket change and popping the coins they found into collecting folders.

Their true riches were the fun they had and the things they learned while collecting coins.

# THE WORLD'S OLDEST COIN

While the first coins were probably made in China, the oldest coins known today come from Lydia (now present-day Turkey) and date between 700-600 B.C. Known as "staters," they were made from a silver and gold "alloy," or mixture. The staters have a lion's head on the obverse, or front, and a punch mark on the reverse. The punch mark comes from the hammer used to engrave the design into the coin. Unlike present-day coins, these coins were made by hand. The staters are smaller than our dime but much thicker, and look like flat pebbles.

---

# A KING, A COIN AND THE CIA:
## *The History of the World's Most Expensive Coin*

In 1933, President Franklin D. Roosevelt ordered that all of the $20 gold coins be collected and melted down in an effort to fix the struggling economy. However, several of these coins escaped being destroyed. One was sold to King Farouk of Egypt, an avid coin collector. When he was dethroned in 1952, the coin was put up for auction. The U.S. asked for it to be withdrawn and handed over. Instead, the coin was removed from the auction but not returned. The coin disappeared for more than 40 years, before it reappeared in New York City in 1996. It was seized by CIA officials posing as coin buyers, and after a lengthy trial, the coin was auctioned off to an anonymous bidder for almost $7.6 million, making it the most expensive coin in the world. You can see two other specimens of this famous coin at the Smithsonian Institution in Washington, D.C.

# CHAPTER
## 2

# SOME EASY THINGS FIRST.

# THEN YOU'RE READY.

It's easy to start collecting coins. There are just a few basic things you need to know first.

### The U.S. Mint makes U.S. coins

The U.S. Mint is the official government agency that makes U.S. coins. It is part of the U.S. Treasury Department. Its headquarters are in Washington, D.C.

The coins are actually produced, however, in several other cities. These coin production facilities are called "mints."

One of them is located in Philadelphia, Pa. The country's first official mint was located there, and the mint located there today is often called the "main mint."

There are also official government mints in Denver, Colo.; San Francisco, Calif.; and West Point, N.Y. These other mints are called "branch mints."

### Coins have dates

The date on a coin is the year in which the coin was produced.

### Coins sometimes have mintmarks

A mintmark is a small letter on the coin that tells you which mint produced the coin. The following mintmarks can be found on U.S. coins:

"P" for Philadelphia
"D" for Denver
"S" for San Francisco
"W" for West Point
U.S. coins without mintmarks were produced at Philadelphia.

 The "obverse" is the heads side, or front side, of a coin. For example, the obverse of the half dollar is the side that pictures John F. Kennedy.

**WORD TO KNOW:** ▷ REVERSE ▷ The "reverse" is the tails side, or back side, of a coin. For example, the reverse of the half dollar is the side that pictures an eagle.

**WORD TO KNOW:** ▷ DENOMINATION ▷ "Denomination" means the coin's face value: 1 cent, 5 cents, 10 cents, 25 cents, 50 cents, or $1.

**WORD TO KNOW:** ▷ CIRCULATION ▷ When coins are spent in daily use, they are said to "circulate." That's because they pass from one person to another. For example, if you buy something for 50 cents at a store, your two quarters go in the store's cash register. When another person buys something at the store, he or she might get the two quarters you spent in change. That person, in turn, might take those two quarters and use them to pay for something at another store. And on and on.

Coins that are produced for this kind of daily use are called "circulation coinage."

# HOW TO MAKE MONEY – LOTS OF IT

The four U.S. Mints make billions of coins a year. How do they do it?

### It starts with an artist

For a new coin, such as the National Parks quarters, artists working at the Philadelphia Mint first draw a picture of what the new coin will look like. They might draw several different pictures for a new coin, so U.S. Mint officials can have several choices from which to choose a new design.

Artists' designs for a medal honoring the United States Infantry.

## A die is made

Through a series of steps and with the help of machines and computers, the design is transferred to a "die."

A die is shaped kind of like a small soda can with the coin design on top. But if you looked down on a die, everything in the design would be backward. For example, draw a simple picture on a sheet of paper and then hold it up to a mirror. See how your picture looks backward in the mirror? That's how the coin design looks on a die. Why? We'll get to that in a moment.

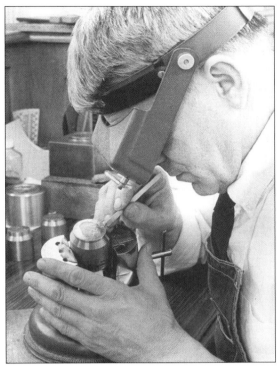

An engraver working on a coin die

## Blanks are made

Large rolls of metal are run through machines that stamp out "blanks." A blank is a round piece of metal the size of a coin, but it has no design on it. It is blank. Blanks are also sometimes called "planchets."

The life expectancy of a circulating coin is 30 years.

A bin full of blanks.

## It all comes together on a coin press

At the mint, the blanks are fed into a coin press. The press takes a die for the obverse of the coin and a die for the reverse of the coin and slams them against the blank – one on each side – at the same time. This presses the design into the blank.

When the backward design on the die is slammed against the blank, the design comes out correctly on the blank.

This process is called "striking." A finished coin has been "struck."

The Mint once considered producing doughnut-shaped coins.

A row of modern coin presses.

## It all happens in the blink of an eye

The whole process – feeding a blank into the press and striking it with the dies – happens in the blink of an eye. All of the mints together can produce millions of coins a day.

## Off to the banks

The presses dump the finished coins into large bins. From the bins, the coins are dumped into bags. The bags of coins are then shipped to banks, who can supply them to businesses and individuals.

Shiny new 1 cent coins.

# MAKE YOUR OWN
## COIN DIE *(sort of)*

Here's another way to see how coin dies work:

1. Find a newer quarter with nice, sharp detail in its design. (Make sure it's a coin that you don't want to save for your collection.)

2. Place a small piece of aluminum foil over it.

3. Press the foil lightly over the coin and hold it so it won't slip.

4. Take the eraser end of a pencil and rub the eraser over the foil. Watch how the coin's design starts to show through the foil.

5. When the whole design shows through the foil, carefully lift the foil off the coin.

6. Look on the other side of the foil – the inside part that was pressed against the coin. See how the design appears backward on the inside part of the foil? Notice, too, how the raised parts of the design on the coin, such as the lettering, look indented on the foil.

That's how the design looks on a coin die. If you could take your aluminum foil "die" and press it hard enough into some soft surface, the design would come out forward-facing on the surface.

## Coins get grades

As a coin circulates, its design starts to wear down from being handled. Line up three or four Lincoln cents from a pocketful of change and you can see that some are more worn than others. On 1 cent coins, this can be seen especially in the detail in Lincoln's hair.

Circulating Lincoln cents with different amounts of wear.

Over the years, the coin collecting hobby has come up with some terms to describe a coin's condition, or how much wear is on the coin. These terms are called "grades."

A coin with no wear is called "uncirculated." A coin with only slight wear on the highest points of its design is graded "extremely fine." A coin with more wear in its design is graded "very fine." A coin with lots of wear is graded "very good," even though it's not really very good.

There are entire books on coin grading. As you learn more about coin collecting, it's important to learn more about grading. That's because coins in better condition are worth more to collectors.

Grading isn't as important when collecting coins from pocket change. But here's something you can do that will help you learn about grading.

If you find a coin that you already have in your collection, compare the newly found coin with the one you had before. Check the design details, like Lincoln's hair on a 1 cent coin. A magnifying glass can be a big help when looking at coins.

**The early Philadelphia Mint used horses to run the machines that produced coins.**

Which coin looks better? If so, why? Remember: You're looking for wear on the coin, not necessarily how shiny it is.

After looking at the two coins, keep the one you think is in better condition. Repeating this exercise over and over again will help make you an expert coin grader someday.

## Get a handle on coins

The less collectible coins are handled, the better. Handling leads to wear, and wear leads to lower grades.

Often, however, collectible coins have to be handled, especially when searching pocket change or placing the coin in a folder. When you must handle a collectible coin, hold it by the edges between your thumb and forefinger. Avoid touching it on the obverse and reverse surfaces.

It's also a good idea to handle collectible coins over a soft surface so they won't be damaged if dropped accidentally.

Hold a coin by its edges.

## Don't clean your coins

Trying to clean a coin can actually do more harm than good. That's because cleaning methods are abrasive, which means they can damage a coin's surface and lower a coin's grade.

It's best to leave a coin as you found it.

The Denver Mint produces more coins than any mint in the world.

## Folders make collections

When do a bunch of coins become a collection? When they are sorted by dates and mintmarks, and are inserted into a collecting folder. Folders are the most inexpensive and common form of organizing and storing a collection.

Coin folders have a spot for each date and mintmark of a particular series of coins, such as Lincoln cents. Thus, folders help collectors in several ways:

- They tell you what dates and mintmarks have been issued for a series of coins.
- They organize your collection.

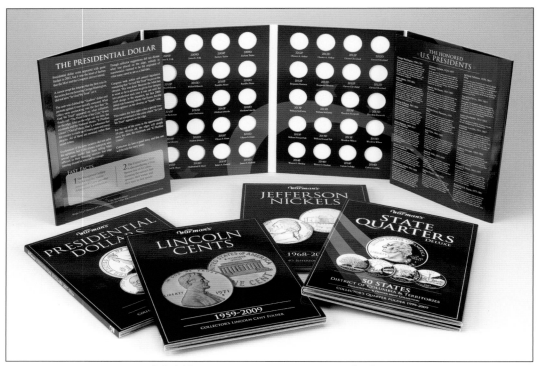

Coin folders are a great way to start your collection.

- They preserve your coins, so they are no longer handled and open to more wear.
- They make your collection easy to store.
- They make your collection easy and enjoyable to look at.

The folders have holes sized specially for a particular series of coins. They are meant to be a tight fit so the coins, once inserted, won't fall out. To insert a coin into the folder, place it in the hole at an angle, so one side of the coin is in the hole. On the side of the coin sticking up, press down and toward the angled side until the coin snaps into place.

If you end up touching the coin's surface to get it in the folder, don't worry. That's OK. Just limit the contact as best you can.

That's it! That's all you need to know to start collecting coins. So let's get started.

# CHAPTER

**3**

# Let's start collecting.

### How to form a coin collection

A coin collection can be pretty much anything you want it to be. For example, one 1 cent coin from each year since the year you were born could be a collection. A coin from each of the years in which members of your family were born can be a collection. There are many possibilities.

Here are some common ways to form collections:

### By date and mintmark

This probably is the most popular way to collect coins. In this method, collectors seek one example of each date and mintmark combination of a particular series. For Lincoln Memorial cents, that would mean one 1959 cent (no mintmark, which means it was produced at the Philadelphia Mint), one 1959-D cent (the "D" mintmark means it was produced at the Denver Mint), one 1960 cent, one 1960-D cent, and so on right through to the present year.

To collect this way, you have to know what dates and mintmarks were issued in a particular series. You can get this information from coin collecting folders, which contain a labeled spot for each date and mintmark combination of a series. You can also get this information from magazines, like *Coin Prices*, and from books that list every date and mintmark combination for different series of coins.

### By type

Before there was a Lincoln Memorial cent, there was a Lincoln cent with wheat ears on the reverse (from 1909 through 1958). Before that, the U.S. cent pictured an Indian on the obverse (from 1859 through 1909). Each of these different designs is a called a "type" in the coin collecting hobby – the Indian type cent, the Lincoln Wheat Ear type cent, and the Lincoln Memorial type cent.

Some collectors seek just one example of each design type. They may focus on just one denomination (1 cent coins or 5-cent coins or quarters), or they may focus on coins from certain years (the 20th century, for example). The advantage to collecting by type is that a coin of any date and mintmark in a series can fill a spot in a collection.

Let's go back to those 1 cent coins for a moment. A type collection of Indian and Lincoln cents would include the following:

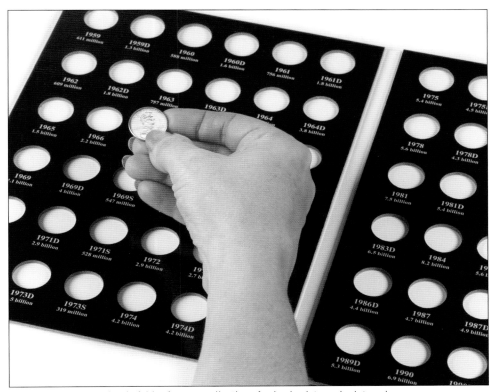

A coin folder forms a collection of coins by date and mintmark

Obverse and reverse of 1877 Indian cent.

Obverse and reverse of 1911-D Lincoln cent.

Obverse and reverse of 1980-S Lincoln cent.

1. Indian cent, can be any date and mintmark
2. Lincoln cent with the wheat ears reverse, can be any date and mintmark
3. Lincoln cent with the Lincoln Memorial reverse, can be any date and mintmark

There are many possibilities for collecting by type. There are many ways to combine denominations, designs, and years to form a collection. The best part is, you get to decide. And if you decide to change the focus of your collection at some point, that's OK too.

### Where to look for coins for your collection

So far, we've talked a lot about simply watching pocket change for coins. And that's still a good way to find coins for a collection. Many older collectors still keep a close watch on their pocket change. They can find coins for current series, such as Lincoln Memorial cents and the National Parks quarters. Older coins, such as Lincoln Wheat Ear cents, sometimes show up in everyday pocket change too.

Be sure to watch your pocket change if your family travels to another part of the country on vacation. Certain dates and mintmarks of a particular series may be hard to find where you live, but they can show up in other parts of the country.

Here are some other ways to find coins for your collection:

### Let friends and relatives know you are collecting

Let them know what coins you want for your collection. For example, let them know if you are collecting Lincoln Memorial cents or the 50 State quarters or the National Parks quarters. And especially let them know if you need a specific date or mintmark of a coin. They may be willing to put aside coins for you as they turn up in their pocket change and then let you look through them later.

### Look through lots of coins when you can

Take advantage of every chance you get to look through a large number of coins. For example, if your family owns a business, can you look through the change in the cash register now and then?

Sometimes people take their pocket change and throw it in a big jar or other container every night. If you have a friend or relative who does this, can you ask them to look through their coins now and then?

# COIN MAGIC

Want a different use for some of the coins left over from searching your bank rolls? Use them to learn some magic tricks.

## THE VANISHING COIN

After showing the audience a coin in your left hand, you enclose your right hand around the coin, and bring it up to your lips. But when you blow open your hand, the coin has disappeared. Where did it go?

With the outside of your left hand facing the audience, hold the coin between your thumb and middle finger so the audience can see it.

Enclose your right hand around your left hand with your palm facing toward you. Your right hand should be more or less perpendicular to your left.

Pretend to grab the coin with your right hand, making a fist. In reality, let the coin slip down into your left palm.

Letting your left hand drop to your side, bring your right hand up to your lips, keeping your eyes focused on this hand. This will draw attention away from your left hand, where the coin really is.

When your right hand reaches your lips, blow into your hand while at the same time opening it up to reveal that the coin has disappeared.

### Just remember ...

Remember two things when you have the chance to look through somebody else's coins: Always ask permission first, and always replace any coins you want to keep. For example, if you find a quarter you want for your collection in a relative's coin jar, always replace it with another quarter.

### Search rolls of coins

Banks store their coins rolled up in specially made paper wrappers. Searching these "rolls" of coins from your local bank is a great way to add coins to your collection. Many older collectors searched rolls in their early collecting days and still do today.

This may require a loan from your mom or dad, because, of course, banks don't give away money. Here's what it costs:

- There are 50 coins in a roll of 1 cent coins. So a roll of 1 cent coins costs 50 cents.
- There are 40 coins in a roll of 5-cent coins. So a roll of 5-cent coins costs $2.
- There are 50 coins in a roll of dimes. So a roll of dimes costs $5.
- There are 40 coins in a roll of quarters. So a roll of quarters costs $10.
- There are 20 coins in a roll of half dollars. So a roll of half dollars costs $10.

As you can see, 50 cents in 1 cent coins cost only 50 cents, and $10 in quarters cost only $10. You don't have to pay anything extra. Also, any coins you don't want to keep can go toward repaying your loan to your mom or dad.

# THE MAGIC GLASS

You have an ordinary coin and an ordinary glass on a white tabletop. Draping a cloth over the glass, you move it on top of the coin. When you remove the cloth, the coin has vanished. How did you do it?

**1** Before your performance, take a sheet of paper and cut out a circle to place over the bottom of the glass. Glue this onto the glass's rim, making sure it covers the whole glass but doesn't overhang.

**2** Place a white tablecloth over the surface you will be performing on. Place the glass on the table, along with a handkerchief or cloth big enough to cover the glass. Gather your audience.

**3** To start, ask your audience for a coin and place it on the table next to the glass. Pick the glass up slightly to show them, but be careful to keep the paper unnoticeable.

**4** Place the handkerchief over the glass. Pick up both and place them over the coin. Take off the handkerchief and show them the coin has disappeared.

**5** Place the handkerchief back over the glass and move it into its original spot. The coin has reappeared.

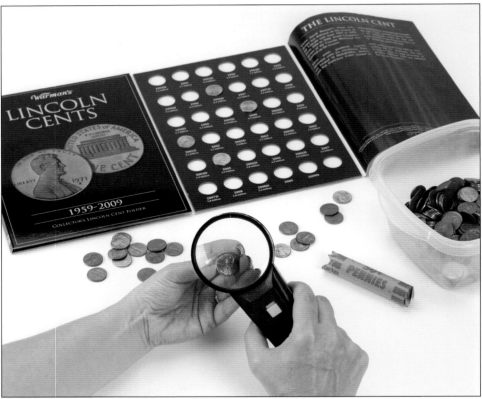
A magnifying glass can help you take a close look at mintmarks and dates.

### How to search through rolls of coins

Besides the rolls of coins, here's what else you'll need to search them:

- A table or desk in a spot with good lighting.
- Something soft to put on the table over the spot where you'll be working. A placemat or small towel will do.
- Your coin folder.
- A plastic jar or other sturdy container in which to put the coins you don't want.
- A magnifying glass can be helpful in reading dates and mintmarks, and checking the condition of a coin.

# THE MYSTERIOUS COIN FOLD

Picking up an ordinary coin, you fold it into an index card before your audience. Then, holding the coin packet in front of you, you rip it completely in half. There is no longer a coin inside. How did that happen?

As you fold the index card in half for the first time, make sure the fold is not even. Leave about a quarter of an inch gap between the two ends.

Fold the card on each of the two ends perpendicular to the first fold. You should now have a little packet with the coin inside. As you fold, press the card around the coin, leaving an impression of the coin on the packet. This will make your act look more convincing.

At this point, you can offer your packet to a member of the audience for verification that the coin is inside. Otherwise, flap the packet around to show the coin cannot slip out.

With your left palm facing toward you, squeeze the packet with your pointer and ring finger while holding it towards your audience with your middle and thumb. This will allow the coin to slide into your palm. Do this quickly and with as little movement as possible.

Next, fold the last end before holding the packet in clear view of the audience, keeping the coin hidden in your palm. Rip the packet in half to reveal it is now empty.

Now let's start searching those rolls:

- Break open a roll and let the coins spill out onto the soft surface you placed over the table or desk. You should be able to just grab the end of the wrapper and unroll it.
- Check Chapter 2 again for the proper way to handle collectible coins.
- As you pick up each coin, check its date and mintmark to see if it fills a spot in your folder.
- If it does, just place the coin over the spot for now. Don't insert it yet.
- If you find another coin of the same date and mintmark, compare it to the one you found before. Which one is in better condition? A magnifying glass can help you check for wear in details in the coin's design, such as the hair on Lincoln's head on the 1 cent coin. Keep the coin that's in better condition, and throw the other one in the discard jar.
- When you're finished searching your roll or rolls, go back and insert your keepers into your folder.

You can take the discard jar back to the bank and exchange the remaining coins for paper money. You don't have to roll the coins up again. Your bank should be able to take the jar and dump the coins into a machine that can count them.

### Watch for valuable silver coins

As you look through coins, watch for dimes, quarters, and half dollars dated before 1965 (1964 and earlier). These coins were made primarily of silver. Starting in 1965, dimes and quarters are made primarily from copper combined with nickel.

The half dollar still contained some silver through 1970. It switched to the copper-nickel composition in 1971.

Here's how much silver is in each pre-1965 coin:

Dime: 0.0724 troy ounces.

Quarter: 0.1809 troy ounces.

Half dollar: 0.3618 troy ounces.

Half dollars dated 1965, 1966, 1967, 1968, 1969 and 1970 contain 0.148 troy ounces of silver.

Obverse and reverse of
1956 Roosevelt dime.

Obverse and
reverse of 1936
Washington
quarter.

Obverse and reverse
of 1964-P Kennedy
half dollar.

It gets harder to find silver coins in pocket change or rolls with each passing year, but they still turn up once in a while. It pays to watch for them.

The price of silver has been high in recent years. In early 2011, it was about $40 for one troy ounce of silver. Current silver prices can be found in many newspapers, including *USA Today*.

### How to find silver prices on the Internet
- Go to www.usatoday.com.
- Click on the word "Markets" at the top of the page.
- Click on the word "Commodities" at the top of the page.
- Scroll down the page until you find the listing for silver.

To determine how much the silver in a pre-1965 coin is worth, multiply the current price of silver by the number of troy ounces of silver in the coin, as listed above.

For example, if the current price of silver is $40 a troy ounce, here's how you would figure the silver value in a pre-1965 quarter, which contains 0.1809 troy ounces of silver:

40 x 0.1809 = 7.23.

If silver is worth $40 a troy ounce, the value of the silver in a pre-1965 quarter would be $7.23.

Many people may not know to watch for these coins. But now you do.

# CHAPTER

## 4

# Money made simple.

# Thank you, Mr. Jefferson.

It's so simple: 100 cents equal 1 dollar.
Even when you break it down further, it stays simple:

1 dime equals 10 cents
10 dimes equal 1 dollar (10 cents x 10)
1 quarter equals 25 cents
4 quarters equal 1 dollar (25 cents x 4)

Any way you slice it, it always comes back to 100 cents equal 1 dollar. But it wasn't always that easy in our country.

## Money in Colonial America

There were few coins in the 13 Colonies, before the United States was formed. Most of the coins that did circulate were coins of other countries that settlers brought with them when they arrived in America. Later on, some of the Colonies and private individuals issued coins.

But for the most part, colonists and their businesses relied on barter, or trading. For example, a farmer might offer a carpenter a certain number of chickens for building a new shed for him. The farmer would get the new shed he needed, and in exchange, the carpenter would get something to eat.

The carpenter, in turn, might have kept some of the chickens he got from the farmer, but he might have traded some of the others. He might have traded one for a sack of flour, another one for some vegetables, and maybe another one for a box of nails or some lumber.

## The country's first coins

When the United States was first formed, states were given the right to issue coins. Some of them did, and the coins were actually used. Coins of other countries also circulated in the new country. Among them were coins of Portugal, Great Britain, France, and Spain.

But the system didn't work well. Some individuals produced fakes of the state and foreign coins. And different states valued the coins differently. Imagine if you traveled to a different state today and the quarter in your pocket wasn't worth 25 cents in the other state. It might be worth 30 cents, or it might be worth only 20 cents. And if you traveled to yet another state, it might be valued differently there too.

So the country decided that the federal government, not the state governments, should issue coins. That way, the same coins would be used in all the states, and the coins would have the same values in all the states.

### The "most easy" system

Values of the state-issued coins were based on the old British system of pounds, shillings, and pence. Imagine having to learn this system of coin values:

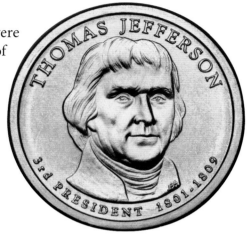

A modern dollar coin honoring Thomas Jefferson

4 farthings equal 1 penny
12 pence equal 1 shilling
2 shillings equal 1 florin
5 shillings equal 1 crown
20 shillings equal 1 pound

Obverse and reverse of 1750 shilling.

Obverse and reverse of 1799 farthing.

Think fast: How many farthings were there in a pound?

To make it even more confusing, the British had nicknames for their coin values:

6 pence were a "tanner"          10 shillings were "half a quid"
A shilling was a "bob"           20 pounds were a "pony"

So when the U.S. government discussed a new coinage system for the country, it focused on decimal systems. In a decimal system, everything is based on units of 10, which are easy to multiply and divide.

Thomas Jefferson took some ideas that had been discussed before, made a few changes to them, and suggested a coinage system for the new country. Our coinage system today – 100 cents equal 1 dollar – is based largely on Jefferson's suggestion.

"The most easy ratio of multiplication and division is that by 10," Jefferson wrote. "Every one knows the facility of Decimal Arithmetic."

Today, most countries use a decimal coinage system. Even Great Britain switched to a decimal system in 1970.

### The new U.S. Mint

The U.S. Congress passed an act establishing the U.S. Mint in April 1792. The act also authorized the following coins:

Obverse and reverse of 1793 half cent.

### Copper
Half cent
Cent

### Silver
Half disme (or half dime, worth 5 cents)
Disme (known as the dime today)
Quarter dollar
Half dollar
Dollar

Obverse and reverse of 1793 cent with wreath reverse.

### Gold
$2.50 (also called a "quarter eagle")
$5 ("half eagle")
$10 ("eagle")

Obverse and reverse of 1792 half disme.

Now the country could start producing official U.S. coinage. The actual production facility, called a "mint," was located in Philadelphia, Pa. In July 1792, it produced a small number of half dismes. A few of these coins still exist today, but they are rare and very valuable.

Coinage began in earnest in 1793. In that year the Philadelphia Mint produced more than 35,000 half cents and more than 100,000 1 cent coins. By

# COINS THAT USED TO BE

Have you seen many half cents in pocket change lately? No? That's because the U.S. Mint stopped producing half cents in 1858. The last year they were produced was 1857.

Here are some other coin denominations that are no longer produced:

### 3 cents

Silver 3-cent coins were produced from 1851 through 1873, and nickel 3-cent coins were produced from 1865 through 1889.

Obverse and reverse of a silver 3-cent coin.

Obverse and reverse of 1877 nickel 3-cent coin.

### 20 cents

These silver coins were produced from 1875 through 1878.

Obverse and reverse of 1876 20-cent coin.

### Gold $3

These coins were produced from 1854 through 1889.

### Half dimes

Silver half dimes, which were worth 5 cents, were first produced in 1794 and last produced in 1873. In 1866, the United States introduced a nickel 5-cent coin.

Obverse and reverse of 1838 half dime.

### Gold $1

Many people are familiar with the old silver dollar coins, but the United States also issued gold dollar coins from 1849 through 1889.

Obverse and reverse of a gold dollar.

Obverse and reverse of 1860-S gold $3 coin.

## DID YOU KNOW?
### *People Facts*

- Only four men have been depicted on a coin during their lifetime: President Calvin Coolidge, a governor of Alabama, and two senators.

- Seven women have appeared on U.S. coinage before the First Spouses Program: Sacagawea, Susan B. Anthony, Helen Keller, Virginia Dare, Queen Isabella of Spain, and Eunice Kennedy Shriver.

- Booker T. Washington was the first African-American to appear on a U.S. coin.

- The first U.S. commemorative coin featured Christopher Columbus in 1892.

1796, the Mint was producing silver and gold coins, too. By the mid-1800s, the U.S. Mint was producing about 20 million coins each year.

### U.S. coins today

U.S. coins have seen many changes over the centuries. The U.S. Mint stopped producing gold coins for circulation in the 1930s. It stopped producing silver coins in 1965. (The dime, quarter, and half dollar today are composed of copper and nickel.) Some new denominations for coins were introduced over the years, but didn't last.

But our coinage system today is still based on the one Mr. Jefferson suggested: 100 cents equal 1 dollar. It's so simple.

# CHAPTER

## 5

# IT MAKES SENSE TO START WITH CENTS.

"What were the first coins you collected?"

Ask any older collector that question, and chances are good they'll say, "Lincoln cents."

Many coin collectors started by searching pocket change and rolls of coins for Lincoln cents. A big reason for that is cost. It costs only 1 cent to add a Lincoln cent from pocket change to your collection. Plus, Abraham Lincoln is an important and now popular figure in American history.

### Think Lincoln cents, think 9

Nine. That's the number to remember when collecting Lincoln cents. Many of the important years for Lincoln cents end in 9.

1809 – Abraham Lincoln, who would become the 16th president of the United States, was born on Feb. 12 in Hardin County, Ky.

1909 – The Lincoln cent was introduced to mark the centennial of Lincoln's birth. It featured Lincoln's portrait on the obverse and the words "One Cent" framed by a pair of wheat ears on the reverse.

1959 – To mark the 150th anniversary of Lincoln's birth, the reverse of the cent was changed to depict the Lincoln Memorial in Washington, D.C.

2009 – To mark the bicentennial of Lincoln's birth, a special series of four 1 cent coins was issued.

### How to collect Lincoln cents

Collecting all of the date and mintmark combinations of Lincoln cents since 1909 is a challenge even for experienced collectors. There is little chance of finding the early dates in pocket change, and many of them are expensive to buy from coin dealers. Some cost thousands of dollars.

Obverse and reverse of
1909 Lincoln cent.

*Heritage Numismatic Auctions images.*

But Lincoln cents with the old wheat ears reverse still show up in pocket change now and then. When you do find one, it's fun to check the date on it and save it. You may find others to add to it and make at least a small collection of Wheat Ear cents.

### Focus on Lincoln Memorial cents

All dates of Lincoln Memorial cents – those issued from 1959 through 2008 – can be found in pocket change. It will take some time and some searching to find them all, but it can be done. And remember, the searching and the eventual finding make up the fun of collecting.

Obverse and reverse of 1959 Lincoln cent.
*Heritage Numismatic Auctions images.*

A collecting folder for Lincoln Memorial cents will tell you what date and mintmark combinations are needed to complete a collection. For most years, Lincoln Memorial cents have either no mintmark (which means they were struck at the Philadelphia Mint) or a "D" mintmark (for the Denver Mint). Lincoln cents for circulation also were struck with an "S" mintmark (for the San Francisco Mint) from 1968 through 1974.

The mintmark on the Lincoln cent can be found under the date on the obverse.

### How to find them

Keep a close watch on your pocket change for a Lincoln Memorial cent that will fill a spot in your folder. Also, ask to look at the 1 cent coins in your mom's and dad's pocket change or the change of other family members.

To fill up your folder faster, get some rolls of 1 cent coins from your local bank. Searching just a few rolls of coins can fill many spots in a Lincoln Memorial cent folder.

See Chapter 3 again for tips on searching rolls of coins.

Obverse of 2009 Lincoln cent.

### Focus on Lincoln Bicentennial cents

In 2009, the U.S. Mint issued some special cents to mark the bicentennial, or 200th anniversary, of Lincoln's birth.

On the obverse, each coin had the portrait of Lincoln used on the 1 cent coin since 1909. But there were four different reverses issued:

Log cabin Lincoln cent reverse.        Lincoln reading reverse.

1. The first reverse depicts a log cabin with the date 1809 below. This reverse symbolizes Lincoln's birth in a log cabin in 1809.

2. The second reverse shows Lincoln sitting on a log and reading a book with an ax at his side. When Lincoln was 8 years old, his family moved to a farm in Indiana. Lincoln loved to read and learn. He would often take a book with him to read during breaks in his farm work.

3. The third reverse shows Lincoln standing in front of Illinois' Old State Capitol. Before he was elected president, Lincoln was elected to the Illinois General Assembly in 1834.

4. The fourth reverse shows the U.S. Capitol in Washington, D.C., with its dome half finished. This is how the Capitol looked when Lincoln was first inaugurated president in 1861. It was completed in 1863. This design symbolizes the nation torn apart by the Civil War during Lincoln's presidency.

### How to find them

A close watch on pocket change and a search of rolls should turn up all of the coins needed to complete a collection of Lincoln Bicentennial cents. Because the coins were issued recently, you should be able to find shiny examples with little wear. Collectors call the shininess "luster."

Illinois Old State Capitol reverse.          U.S. Capitol reverse.

### The current Lincoln cent

Yet another change was made to the Lincoln cent design in 2010. Starting in that year, the reverse design now depicts a union shield. This design symbolizes the preservation of the United States as a single, unified country

# SHOULD IT STAY OR SHOULD IT GO?
## The "Penny" Debate

Should we keep the 1 cent coin or get rid of it? This has been a recent debate in the United States. Because of rising costs in our society, many people argue that the 1 cent coin is no longer useful and costs more to make and support than it is worth. Others feel that eliminating it will make prices only rise further. Many want to keep the coin because of its long history and because it is so familiar. Some other countries, such as New Zealand, Israel, and Brazil, have eliminated their smaller coins. Still other countries, Canada and Japan, for example, continue to use theirs, just as we will do – for now.

following the Civil War.

At the top of the shield is the Latin phrase "E Pluribus Unum," which means "out of many, one." Our country is composed of many states. Living in those states are people of many different backgrounds. But together we form one country.

The motto can be found on other U.S. coins, too.

Union Shield cent reverse.

### Key points for grading

The key areas to check for wear on a Lincoln cent are Lincoln's cheekbone and the detail in his hair.

### Copper no more

Over the years, the Lincoln cent has seen many changes in its composition, the metals from which the coin is produced.

### 1909-1942

The cent was composed mostly of copper and a little bit of tin and zinc.

Obverse of 1964-D Lincoln cent showing two areas to check for wear and mintmark location.

### 1943

In this year, the cent was composed of steel with a thin zinc coating over the top. This was during World War II, and copper was important to manufacturing related to the war effort.

These 1943 steel cents are silvery rather than brown. They still show up in pocket change and rolls of cents now and then, but they are not valuable. They still, however, are worth saving for a collection if you find one.

### 1944-1982

The cent went back to a mostly copper composition with a little bit of zinc. The tin was eliminated.

### 1982-present

Lincoln cents today are composed mostly of zinc with a thin copper plating over the top.

### Where are the "pennies?"

Have you noticed we've yet to call the 1 cent coin a "penny" in this book? That's because officially the U.S. Mint does not issue "pennies." The official denomination, as shown on the coin, is "one cent." A penny is a British coin.

Now, you won't get arrested if you call the U.S. 1 cent coin a penny. Rolls of 1 cent coins from banks are labeled "pennies," and even the U.S. Mint calls them "pennies" on its website (www.usmint.gov).

But listen closely to older collectors and you will always hear them call a 1 cent coin a "cent."

## LOOK THE OTHER WAY

Up until the release of the new Jefferson nickel in 2005, Abraham Lincoln was the only president on a coin to face right. Why is this? When President Theodore Roosevelt chose a design for the Lincoln Centennial Year, he was most impressed with the work of designer Victor David Brenner. Brenner's portrait of Lincoln faced right, and so, that is the direction the former president faces.

## ON THE FLIP SIDE

Look closely at the images of the obverse and reverse of a coin. Coins are designed so that when the obverse is right side up, the reverse is upside down, or flipped. This is called a "coin turn." If both sides have the same orientation, it is called a "medal turn." Even though there is no law or official reason (other than tradition) for doing so, all coins in the U.S. are made with a coin turn orientation.

## Count the Lincolns

Here's a trick question that will trip up a lot of people:

How many images of Lincoln are there on the Lincoln Memorial cent?

To answer this question, get out a Lincoln Memorial cent that still has sharp details in its design.

The portrait of Lincoln on the obverse, of course, counts as one image.

Now flip the coin over and look closely at the reverse. Focus on the middle of the Lincoln Memorial. The design includes an outline representing the statue of Lincoln in the real Lincoln Memorial. A magnifying glass will help you see it.

So the correct answer to the question above is two.

Reverse of Lincoln Memorial cent.

# CHAPTER

## 6

# Step up to Jefferson nickels.

When you're ready to step up from Lincoln cents, consider Jefferson nickels. As collectibles, they're similar to Lincoln cents. Here are some ways they're alike:

- You can still find old Lincoln cents with the wheat ears design in pocket change. And you can still find old Jefferson nickels in pocket change, too. It's not unusual to find Jefferson nickels from the 1960s, '50s, '40s, and even '30s in pocket change or rolls of nickels.
- Yes, Jefferson nickels are each worth 4 cents more than Lincoln cents. But it still doesn't cost much to collect Jefferson nickels from circulation.
- Like Lincoln cents, a special series of Jefferson nickels was issued in recent years. The series is short and can be collected from circulation (pocket change and rolls).

Obverse and reverse of 1918 Buffalo nickel.          Obverse and reverse of 1943 Jefferson nickel.

### The first Jefferson nickels

The first Jefferson nickels were issued in 1938. They replaced the Buffalo nickel, which remains popular with collectors today.

The obverse of the nickel depicts Thomas Jefferson, who was the third U.S. president (1801-1809). The reverse depicts his Virginia home, Monticello.

The Jefferson nickel saw some changes from 1942 through 1945, during World War II. The composition was changed from copper-nickel to copper, silver, and manganese. To mark the change, the mintmark was moved from below the date on the obverse to above the dome on Monticello on the reverse.

### How to collect Jefferson nickels

Older Jefferson nickels can still be found in pocket change and rolls of coins. In fact, it may be easier to find older dates of Jefferson nickels than it

Examples of older Jefferson nickels that can still be found in circulation.

is to find older dates of any other coin series.

They are a couple of reasons for this:

- There were no changes in the Jefferson nickel design for many years. So older dates don't stand out in pocket change as they do for some other coin series. For example, the reverse of the Lincoln cent changed from the wheat ears design on the reverse to the Lincoln Memorial design in 1959. When people notice the wheat ears design in pocket change, they notice that it's an older coin and maybe put it aside.

- Except for the nickels of 1942-1945, the composition of the Jefferson nickel has not changed since it was introduced in 1938. Until 1965, dimes, quarters, and half dollars were composed mostly of silver. When people notice a pre-1965 coin (1964 and earlier) in their pocket change, they usually put it aside because silver is valuable today.

The mottoes "E Pluribus Unum" and "In God We Trust" appear on every circulating coin since 1908.

Paul Revere once supplied the Mint with copper for its early cents.

A collector folder will tell you what dates and mintmarks were issued for Jefferson nickels. It takes some searching, and some will be harder to find than others. But it's possible to find all dates and mintmarks of Jefferson nickels in circulation.

But be patient. It's not something you'll do over a weekend. Just check the dates and mintmarks on nickels whenever you get the chance, and one by one you'll see the holes in your folder fill up.

### Focus on Westward Journey nickels

In 2004 and 2005, the U.S. Mint issued a special series of nickels called the Westward Journey series. The nickels were issued to mark the 200th anniversary of the Louisiana Purchase and the exploration of the American West by Lewis and Clark.

The Louisiana Purchase was one of the most important acts of Jefferson's presidency. In 1803, Jefferson paid France about $15 million for more than 800,000 square miles of land. The additional land about doubled the size of the United States.

The land included all or part of the following current states: Arkansas, Colorado, Iowa, Kansas, Louisiana, Minnesota, Missouri, Montana, Nebraska, North Dakota, Oklahoma, South Dakota, Texas, and Wyoming.

In 1804, Jefferson chose Meriwether Lewis and William Clark to head an expedition to explore some of the new land. They left from St. Louis, Mo., in

Obverse and reverse of
2004 peace medal nickel.

the spring of 1804. They headed up the Missouri River and explored parts of present-day Iowa, Nebraska, North Dakota, South Dakota, and Montana. Eventually, they went all the way west to the Pacific Ocean. They arrived there in November 1805.

### The Westward Journey designs

There are four different reverse designs in the Westward Journey nickel series:

### 1. Peace medal design

Lewis and Clark carried a number of specially made medals on their journey. They gave the medals to Native American chiefs they met along the way. The medal's design was meant to symbolize friendship between the United States and the Native Americans.

The medal's reverse showed two clasped hands. The wrist of one hand is adorned with the cuff of a military uniform. The wrist of the other hand is adorned with beads and a stylized American eagle.

This clasped-hands design was used for the reverse of the first Westward Journey nickel, issued in 2004. The obverse of this coin depicts the portrait of Jefferson that had been used since the Jefferson nickel's introduction.

### 2. Keelboat design

This design depicts the type of watercraft Lewis and Clark used in their travels up the Missouri River.

Reverse of 2004 keelboat nickel.

Two figures in uniforms in the boat's bow represent the two explorers.

This design was also issued in 2004. The obverse also depicts the portrait of Jefferson used on the Jefferson nickel since its introduction.

### 3. Bison design

This design depicts a bison on the nickel's reverse. The bison is commonly called a buffalo. The design is similar to the one used on the Buffalo nickel, which was issued from 1913 through 1938.

This design was chosen for the Westward Journey nickels because Lewis and Clark saw many bison on their explorations. The animal was also important to Native Americans. It pro-

Obverse and reverse of 2005 bison nickel.

# CALLING ALL ARTISTS
## *The Artistic Infusion Project & Designing Coins*

In 2003, the U.S. Mint started a new program known as the Artistic Infusion Project. The AIP, as it is called, has designed for the Presidential Dollars series, the First Spouse coins, the 50 State Quarters series and other programs. There are two levels in the program, Master Designer and Associate Designer, as well as an internship program for college students. Once a design is chosen, one of the Mint's sculptor-engravers (who often design coins as well) sculpts a clay model. Plaster is then poured over the model, to make a negative version that is eventually transferred onto a steel die. The sculptor-engravers all work at the Philadelphia Mint, the only mint where designs are engraved. On the other hand, AIP designers live all over the country. You can find the designer's initials on each coin, although you will often need a magnifying glass to find them.

Obverse and reverse of 2005 "Ocean in view!" nickel.

vided them with food, and its hide was used for making clothing.

The bison design was issued in 2005. Jefferson was still depicted on the obverse, but a different design was used. It showed a partial view of Jefferson's face rather than the usual full view.

### 4. "Ocean in view!" design

This design shows a view of the Pacific Ocean. The words "Ocean in view!" are based on an entry from William Clark's journal. On Nov. 7, 1805, he wrote, "We are in view of the opening of the Ocean, which Creates great joy."

This design was also issued in 2005. It uses the same obverse portrait of Jefferson found on the 2005 nickel with the bison reverse.

### The Jefferson nickel today

In 2006, the Jefferson nickel reverse went back to the original image of Monticello. But the obverse portrait of Jefferson was changed. It now shows Jefferson looking right at you when you look at the coin.

The new image is based on a portrait of Jefferson painted in 1800, right before he became president. Jefferson was 57 years old at the time.

Obverse and reverse of 2011 Jefferson nickel.

## Why a "nickel?"

OK, so the U.S. Mint doesn't officially issue "pennies," and it doesn't officially issue "nickels" either. Officially, they are 5-cent coins.

And there's more copper in a nickel than there is nickel.

So why is a nickel called a nickel?

The first copper-nickel 5-cent coin was issued in 1866. The coin's silvery gray color probably made the nickel in its composition more obvious than the copper.

Also, at that time, the United States still issued a 5-cent coin composed of silver and called a half dime. So the copper-nickel 5-cent coin was commonly called a "nickel" to distinguish it from the silver 5-cent coin.

Oh, by the way, today, everybody calls the current 5-cent coin a "nickel." So you can, too.

The grooves on the edges of certain coins are called "reeds" and were used to prevent counterfeiting. When the coins were made of precious metals, the shavings were sold or reused.

## Check the steps

On Jefferson nickels that picture Monticello on the reverse, a key area to check for wear are the steps on Monticello. They appear under the building's door. A magnifying glass is pretty much required to see them clearly.

When new, nickels will show four distinct lines that represent the steps. Collectors call these "full-step" nickels. They are especially important when grading older, uncirculated nickels.

As the coin wears, the steps look less sharp. Sometimes, even when the coin is new, the steps aren't as sharp as they should be because the press didn't strike them completely.

On the obverse, key points to look for wear are Jefferson's cheekbone and the details in his hair on coins with the original portrait of Jefferson.

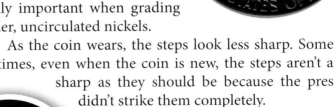

The Philadelphia Mint covers a total of five acres. The present building is the fourth to be built.

Past mints have been located in Georgia, North Carolina, Nevada and Louisiana.

# CHAPTER

# DIME TIME.

The Roosevelt dime seems over-looked at times as a collectible coin. But it is an important part of our coinage system and can be an exciting step in developing your coin collecting interest.

## To honor a president

The Roosevelt dime was first issued in 1946 as a tribute to the late President Franklin Delano Roosevelt. "FDR," as he is commonly called, was first elected president in 1932. He won re-election in 1936, 1940, and 1944. He is the only president in U.S.

President Franklin D. Roosevelt.

history to serve more than two terms. (Current law prevents a president from serving more than two terms.)

Roosevelt served during some difficult times in our nation's history. The 1930s were the time of the Great Depression. The economy was poor during this time. Many businesses closed, and others struggled to stay open. As a result, many people couldn't find work, and it was difficult for them to support their families.

Then, in 1941, the United States entered World War II. Factories and other business were put to work again producing equipment and supplies needed for the war effort, such as trucks and airplanes. This helped revive the economy.

But many young men were called to serve in the Army and Navy, and many lost their lives in the war.

## Why the dime

The war was still going on when Roosevelt died on April 12, 1945, although it would end later that year. Discussions about honoring Roosevelt on a coin began soon after his death.

Congress must approve changing any coin design that has been used for less than 25 years.

Obverse and reverse of 1946 Roosevelt dime.

Obverse and reverse of 1964 Roosevelt dime.

Obverse and reverse of 1968 Roosevelt dime.

At the time of Roosevelt's death, the cent, dime, and half dollar could be redesigned without Congress' approval.

In 1938, Roosevelt established the National Foundation for Infantile Paralysis. The foundation's purpose was to raise money to find a cure for infantile paralysis, which is commonly called polio. Roosevelt himself suffered from the disease for much of his adult life, and it was difficult for him to walk.

People were encouraged to donate dimes to the foundation. This fund-raising effort became known as the March of Dimes. Thus, when Roosevelt died, the dime was chosen as a fitting tribute to the former president.

### The big change in change

The same design for the Roosevelt dime introduced in 1946 is still used today. But in 1965, an important change was made to the coin.

Until that year, the dime – along with the quarter and half dollar – were composed mostly of silver. By the early 1960s, however, the price of silver was increasing. It got to the point where it cost the U.S. Mint more than 10 cents to produce a dime (and more than 25 cents to produce a quarter and more than 50 cents to produce a half dollar).

So in 1965, the Mint changed the composition of the dime, quarter, and half dollar. Today, the coins are composed of a pure-copper core with a copper and nickel cladding over the top.

Because of the change, people started to save the pre-1965 silver coins instead of spending them. In following years, many were sold for their silver content. As a result, it's difficult today to find pre-1965 dimes, quarters, and half dollars in circulation.

### But you can still collect Roosevelt dimes

Do not fret, though. Roosevelt dimes can still be collected from circulation. But the easiest way to collect them is to focus on coins dated 1965 and later – those with the clad composition.

A careful watch on pocket change and searching rolls of coins should fill many of the holes in a coin collecting folder.

The mintmark on 1965 and later Roosevelt dimes is located on the obverse, just above the date.

The key areas to check for wear are Roosevelt's cheekbone and the hair just above his ear.

### Taking the next step

Roosevelt dimes can provide an exciting introduction to the next step in coin collecting: buying coins from dealers. Many coins that you can't

## WHAT'S ON THE BACK?

The reverse of a Roosevelt dime features a torch, olive branch, and oak branch. The torch is meant to symbolize independence, the olive branch represents peace, while the oak represents strengh and independence. Can you tell which is which?

find in pocket change and rolls can be purchased from coin dealers.

These dealers buy and sell collectible coins for a living. Some of them have shops with regular business hours. Others set up at coin shows.

These dealers often have bins piled full of inexpensive coins in cardboard 2-by-2 holders. These bins are commonly called "junk boxes," but they deserve a better name, because their contents aren't junk. So we'll call them "bargain bins."

You can usually find Roosevelt dimes in bargain bins. Uncirculated clad-composition dimes (dated 1965 and later) can be found in bargain bins for $1 to $2 each.

Even silver Roosevelt dimes (1964 and earlier) can be found in bargain bins. Many of them can also be purchased for low cost in high circulated grades or even lower uncirculated grades.

Bargain bins can be a lot of fun. Don't be afraid to get your hands in there and dig for that coin you need.

### What's a silver dime worth?

It gets harder and harder every year to find silver coins (dimes, quarters, and half dollars dated 1964 and earlier) in circulation, especially with the price of silver going through the roof in recent years. But they still show up once in a while. So it's worth it to check the dates on these coins, especially when searching rolls of coins.

A silver dime contains 0.0724 troy ounces of silver. If silver is trading at $40 a troy ounce, a silver dime is worth about $2.90 (0.0724 x 40).

### The case of the missing mintmark

All circulating 1982 dimes are supposed to have a mintmark – either a "P" for Philadelphia or a "D" for Denver. So imagine the excitement among coin collectors in early 1983 when people started finding 1982 dimes without mintmarks.

What happened?

From 1968 through 1979, Roosevelt dimes produced at the Philadelphia Mint did not have a mint mark. Beginning in 1980, the "P" mintmark was added to Roosevelt dimes produced at Philadelphia.

Maybe the Philadelphia Mint workers were too used to producing coins without a mintmark for so many years. Whatever the reason, a die without a "P" mintmark was put on the coining presses in 1982. Apparently, it was some time before somebody noticed the mistake.

Mint mark
1968-present

1982 No mint mark

The result was a number of 1982 Roosevelt dimes produced without a mintmark.

By now, most have probably been pulled from circulation and saved by collectors. But it's possible some are still out there waiting to be discovered by a sharp-eyed and knowing collector. That collector could be you, now that you know to watch for them.

If you do find one, a 1982 dime with no mintmark is worth about $25 to $50 in typical circulated grades. Handle it by the edges, and put it in either a cardboard 2-by-2 holder or plastic "flip" as soon as possible.

Now, remember: Roosevelt dimes struck at the Philadelphia Mint from 1968 through 1979 are not supposed to have mintmarks. So those dates without mintmarks are not rare. It is only the 1982-dated dime without a mintmark that is in error.

### Replacing a legend

The Roosevelt dime replaced the so-called Mercury dime, which is popular among collectors today. The Mercury dime was first issued in 1916 and was produced through 1945. Some dates of Mercury dimes are worth thousands of dollars in top condition.

Some coin books and magazines more correctly call the Mercury dime

## WHAT'S IN A NAME

The dime used to be called a "disme," a French word from the 1500s meaning "one-tenth." It was based on the Latin word "decimus."

Obverse and reverse
of 1942 Mercury
dime.

the Winged Liberty dime. On the coin's obverse, Liberty is represented as a female figure. She is wearing a cap with wings, which is meant to symbolize liberty of thought.

The design reminded some of the ancient god Mercury, who was sometimes pictured wearing a winged hat. Thus, the Winged Liberty dime was nicknamed the Mercury dime.

Today, Mercury dimes sometimes, though rarely, show up in rolls of dimes. Most found this way will be well worn and not especially valuable. But it's still fun to find one, and they're worth putting aside and preserving in a cardboard 2-by-2 holder.

# CHAPTER

## 8

# COLLECT THE QUARTERS THAT CHANGED EVERYTHING.

The U.S. Mint's 50 State quarters program changed everything. For many years, collecting coins from pocket change meant collecting different dates and mintmarks of the same design. Collecting by date and mintmark is still a popular and fun part of the hobby.

But when the 50 State quarters series started in 1999, it created a new way to collect coins from pocket change. Now collectors could look for different designs within a series.

The program was a big hit. The Mint estimated that 147 million people collected the 50 State quarters.

The program was so successful that new quarter programs were started after the 50 State Quarters ended in 2008. In 2009, quarters were issued to honor the District of Columbia and the five U.S. territories. In 2010, the Mint started a series called the America the Beautiful quarters. This series honors national parks and other national sites.

### They're the law

Congress passed laws authorizing each of the quarters program. Each law says the coins should depict George Washington on the obverse. The coins use the same portrait shown on the Washington quarter since it was first issued in 1932.

The reverse designs are different, to honor the subject of each coin. Each law says the coins' reverses cannot have a "frivolous or inappropriate design." It also says the coins' reverses cannot depict a living person, and they cannot depict a head-and-shoulders portrait of any person, living or dead.

### From Delaware to Hawaii

The 50 State quarters program started in 1999 and ended in 2008. Each of the 50 states were honored on a quarter during the program.

The states were honored in the order in which they approved the U.S. Constitution or were admitted to the union. Thus, the first states honored, in 1999, were Delaware, Pennsylvania, New Jersey, Georgia, and Connecticut. The last states honored, in 2008, were Oklahoma, New Mexico, Arizona, Alaska, and Hawaii.

Five states were honored during each year of the program. The U.S. Mint worked with the governor of each state to choose a design to represent their state.

# WHAT WAS THE FIRST NATIONAL PARK?

Yellowstone National Park claims to be America's first national park. But Hot Springs National Park was the first to be honored on an America the Beautiful quarter as America's oldest national park.

So which is correct? They both are.

Hot Springs National Park first came under federal protection in 1832. But it was not officially named a national park until 1921. Before that, it was called a "federal reservation."

Yellowstone National Park first came under federal protection in 1872, 40 years after Hot Springs. But Yellowstone was officially named a national park right from the start, 49 years before Hot Springs was named a national park.

So, Hot Springs is, indeed, "America's oldest national park." And Yellowstone is, indeed, "America's first national park."

---

# LET'S FLIP A COIN

The coin toss has long been a way to solve disputes and ties. The Ancient Romans called it "Navia aut Caput" (Ship or Head), and the Medieval English knew it as "Cross and Pile," both referencing the images on their coins' obverses and reverses.

Coin tossing is often used at the beginning of many sporting events, including football, soccer and cricket. Other sports, such as baseball and fencing, will use a coin toss to break a tie.

Coin tossing has also been used to determine more longlasting decisions. Portland, Ore., was named after the two founders flipped a coin to determine whose hometown would be used to name the new city. The New Zealand lottery uses a coin toss to determine whether the winner receives a bonus winning. Certain countries, such as Canada and Great Britain, even resort to a coin toss to pronounce the winning political candidate if the votes are tied.

## Meet the District of Columbia and five U.S. territories

Thanks to the success of the 50 State quarters program, another series of quarters was issued in 2009. The series kicked off with a coin honoring the District of Columbia.

The series continued with coins honoring the five U.S. territories. These territories are part of the United States. Each territory has its own internal government, similar to a state's government. But the federal U.S. government has authority over each territory's external matters, such as relations with other states and countries.

Residents of these territories are U.S. citizens, but they cannot vote for president in the general election. Some of the territories do elect a representative to the U.S. Congress, but the representative is not allowed to vote on laws.

**DISTRICT OF COLUMBIA** The District of Columbia is home to the U.S. capital, Washington, D.C. It is not part of a state. Instead, it is governed by the federal government.

The District of Columbia quarter depicts musician Duke Ellington on the reverse. Ellington was born in Washington in 1899 and began his career in music there. He was known as the leader of a popular jazz band and as a composer. He died in 1974.

**PUERTO RICO** Puerto Rico is located in the Caribbean Sea, southeast of Florida. It became part of the United States under terms of a treaty that ended the Spanish-American War in 1898.

It officially became a U.S. territory in 1917 and a U.S. commonwealth in 1952. The territory has its own internal government, similar to a state. But the U.S. federal government has authority over its external matters, such as relations with other states and countries, and defense.

The reverse of the Puerto Rico quarter depicts a sentry box from Fort San Felipe del Marro, which was built in the 1500s. It also depicts a hibiscus flower. The phrase "Isla del Encanto" on the quarter means "Island of Enchantment."

**GUAM**  Guam is an island located in the southern Pacific Ocean, about 3,700 miles southwest of Hawaii. It also became part of the United States under terms of a treaty that ended the Spanish-American War in 1898.

The reverse of the Guam quarter depicts a map of the island. In the upper left is a flying proa, a type of boat used for centuries by Guam's native Chamorro people.

On the lower right is a "latte," which is a stone pillar upon which the Chamorro people built their houses centuries ago. Rows of latte pillars can still be seen in Guam.

The phrase "Guahan I Tanó ManChamorro" on the coin means "Guam – Land of the Chamorro."

**AMERICAN SAMOA**  American Samoa consists of five islands in the southern Pacific Ocean, about halfway between Hawaii and New Zealand. It is the only U.S. land that lies south of the equator. American Samoa became part of the United States under terms of an 1899 treaty among the United States, Great Britain, and Germany.

The American Samoa quarter depicts items used in a traditional "ava" ceremony. The ceremony is used to welcome special visitors to the land. Today, it is also used at special occasions, such as weddings.

The phrase "Samoa Muamua Le Atua" on the coin means "Samoa, God is First."

**U.S. VIRGIN ISLANDS**  The U.S. Virgin Islands are located where the Caribbean Sea meets the Atlantic Ocean, about 1,100 miles southeast of Florida. It consists of three main islands and many other smaller islands.

The United States purchased the territory from Denmark in 1917 for $25 million in gold coins. At the time, it was known as the Danish West Indies.

The reverse of the U.S. Virgin Islands quarter depicts a bananaquit, which is the territory's official bird. It also depicts the yellow cedar, which is the territory's official flower.

A map of the three main islands appears above the motto "United in Pride and Hope."

**NORTHERN MARIANA ISLANDS** ▷ The Northern Mariana Islands are located in the northern Pacific Ocean, about 3,800 miles west of Hawaii. The territory consists of 14 islands.

Because of their location, the islands were of great importance during World War II. Japan had controlled the islands since 1914. In the summer of 1944, U.S. forces invaded the islands and gained control after fierce fighting.

After the war, the islands were designated a United Nations trust territory under U.S. administration. In the 1970s, the Northern Mariana people voted to become a U.S. territory. That vote took effect on March 24, 1976.

The Northern Mariana Islands quarter also depicts a latte pillar and a traditional watercraft.

## And now, America the Beautiful Quarters

The start of the America the Beautiful quarters series means there will be new collectible quarters in circulation for many years to come.

The program will honor a national park or national site in each of the 50 states, the District of Columbia, and the five U.S. territories. Five new coins will be issued in each year. The program started in 2010 and will conclude in 2021.

The parks and sites are being honored in the order in which they became owned by the federal government.

Following is a list of the parks and sites to be honored, the states in which they are located, and the year in which they became owned by the federal government:

## 2010

| Location | Site | Established |
|----------|------|-------------|
| Arkansas | Hot Springs National Park | 1832 |
| Wyoming | Yellowstone National Park | 1872 |
| California | Yosemite National Park | 1890 |
| Arizona | Grand Canyon National Park | 1893 |
| Oregon | Mount Hood National Forest | 1893 |

## 2011

| Location | Site | Established |
| --- | --- | --- |
| Pennsylvania | Gettysburg National Military Park | 1895 |
| Montana | Glacier National Park | 1897 |
| Washington | Olympic National Park | 1897 |
| Mississippi | Vicksburg National Military Park | 1899 |
| Oklahoma | Chickasaw National Recreation Area | 1902 |

## 2012

| Location | Site | Established |
| --- | --- | --- |
| Puerto Rico | El Yunque National Forest | 1903 |
| New Mexico | Chaco Culture National Historical Park | 1907 |
| Maine | Acadia National Park | 1916 |
| Hawaii | Hawai'i Volcanoes National Park | 1916 |
| Alaska | Denali National Park | 1917 |

## 2013

| Location | Site | Established |
| --- | --- | --- |
| New Hampshire | White Mountain National Forest | 1918 |
| Ohio | Perry's Victory & International Peace Memorial | 1919 |
| Nevada | Great Basin National Park | 1922 |
| Maryland | Fort McHenry National Monument | 1925 |
| South Dakota | Mount Rushmore National Memorial | 1925 |

## 2014

| Location | Site | Established |
| --- | --- | --- |
| Tennessee | Great Smoky Mountains National Park | 1926 |
| Virginia | Shenandoah National Park | 1926 |
| Utah | Arches National Park | 1929 |
| Colorado | Great Sand Dunes National Park | 1932 |
| Florida | Everglades National Park | 1934 |

## 2015

| Location | Site | Established |
| --- | --- | --- |
| Nebraska | Homestead National Monument of America | 1936 |
| Louisiana | Kisatchie National Forest | 1936 |
| North Carolina | Blue Ridge Parkway | 1936 |
| Delaware | Bombay Hook National Wildlife Refuge | 1937 |
| New York | Saratoga National Historical Park | 1938 |

## 2016

| Location | Site | Established |
| --- | --- | --- |
| Illinois | Shawnee National Forest | 1939 |
| Kentucky | Cumberland Gap National Historical Park | 1940 |
| West Virginia | Harpers Ferry National Historical Park | 1944 |
| North Dakota | Theodore Roosevelt National Park | 1946 |
| South Carolina | Fort Moultrie (Fort Sumter Nat'l Monument) | 1948 |

## 2017

| Location | Site | Established |
| --- | --- | --- |
| Iowa | Effigy Mounds National Monument | 1949 |
| Washington, D.C. | Frederick Douglass Nat'l Historic Site | 1962 |
| Missouri | Ozark National Scenic Riverways | 1964 |
| New Jersey | Ellis Island Nat'l Monument (Statue of Liberty) | 1965 |
| Indiana | George Rogers Clark National Historical Park | 1966 |

## 2018

| Location | Site | Established |
| --- | --- | --- |
| Michigan | Pictured Rocks National Lakeshore | 1966 |
| Wisconsin | Apostle Islands National Lakeshore | 1970 |
| Minnesota | Voyageurs National Park | 1971 |
| Georgia | Cumberland Island National Seashore | 1972 |
| Rhode Island | Block Island National Wildlife Refuge | 1973 |

## 2019

| Location | Site | Established |
| --- | --- | --- |
| Massachusetts | Lowell National Historical Park | 1978 |
| Northern Mariana Islands | American Memorial Park | 1978 |
| Guam | War in the Pacific Nat'l Historical Park | 1978 |
| Texas | San Antonio Missions National Historical Park | 1978 |
| Idaho | Frank Church-River of No Return Wilderness | 1980 |

## 2020

| Location | Site | Established |
| --- | --- | --- |
| American Samoa | National Park of American Samoa | 1988 |
| Connecticut | Weir Farm National Historic Site | 1990 |
| U.S. Virgin Islands | Salt River Bay National Historical Park | 1992 |
| Vermont | Marsh-Billings-Rockefeller National Historical Park | 1992 |
| Kansas | Tallgrass Prairie National Preserve | 1996 |

## 2021

| Location | Site | Established |
| --- | --- | --- |
| Alabama | Tuskegee Airmen National Historic Site | 1998 |

### How to collect them

A collecting folder and a close watch on pocket change are all that are needed to collect the 50 State quarters, the District of Columbia and U.S. territories quarters, and the America the Beautiful quarters. The folder will tell you the coins that were issued in each year. To speed up the search, get some rolls of quarters from your local bank.

Each of these circulating quarters was issued with a "P" mintmark for the Philadelphia Mint and a "D" mintmark for the Denver Mint. Some collectors look for just one example of each quarter and don't care if it has a "P" or "D" mintmark. Others, however, like the challenge of trying to find an example of each quarter with each mintmark. For example, they'll look for a "P" and a "D" of the Connecticut quarter, a "P" and a "D" of the Pennsylvania quarter, and so on right through to the Hawaii quarter.

# America the Beautiful Quarters

**2010-2011 QUARTERS PICTURED**

2010: Arkansas

2010: Wyoming

2010: California

2010: Arizona

2010: Oregon

2011: Pennsylvania

2011: Montana

2011: Washington

2011: Mississippi

2011: Oklahoma

# STATE QUARTERS
1999-2008

1999: Delaware

1999: Pennsylvania

1999: New Jersey

1999: Georgia

1999: Connecticut

2000: Massachusetts

2000: Maryland

2000: South Carolina

2000: New Hampshire

2000: Virginia

2001: New York

2001: North Carolina

# STATE QUARTERS
1999-2008

2001: Rhode Island

2001: Vermont

2001: Kentucky

2002: Tennessee

2002: Ohio

2002: Louisiana

2002: Indiana

2002: Mississippi

2003: Illinois

2003: Alabama

2003: Maine

2003: Missouri

# STATE QUARTERS

### 1999-2008

2003: Arkansas

2004: Michigan

2004: Florida

2004: Texas

2004: Iowa

2004: Wisconsin

2005: California

2005: Minnesota

2005: Oregon

2005: Kansas

2005: West Virginia

2006: Nevada

# STATE QUARTERS

1999-2008

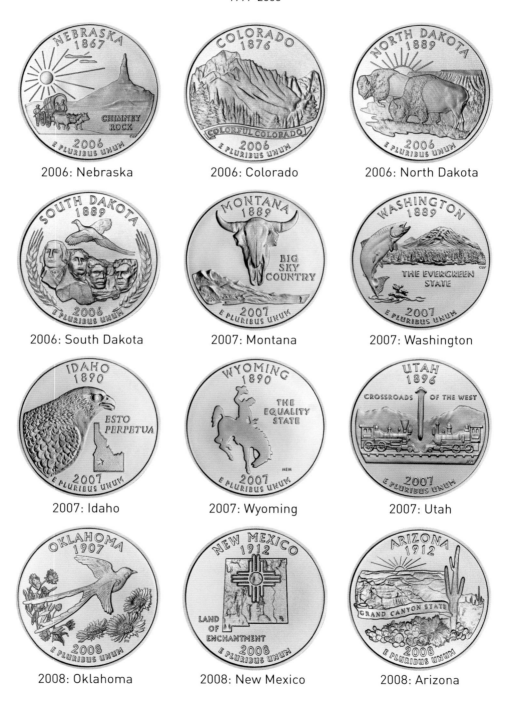

2006: Nebraska

2006: Colorado

2006: North Dakota

2006: South Dakota

2007: Montana

2007: Washington

2007: Idaho

2007: Wyoming

2007: Utah

2008: Oklahoma

2008: New Mexico

2008: Arizona

# State Quarters

1999-2008

2008: Alaska

2008: Hawaii

# District of Columbia & U.S. Territories Quarters

2009

2009: District of Columbia

2009: Puerto Rico

2009: Guam

2009: American Samoa

2009: U.S. Virgin Islands

2009: Northern
Mariana Islands

# CHAPTER
## 9

# HALF DOLLAR MILESTONES MEAN LOTS TO COLLECT.

The Kennedy half dollar is one of the most interesting series of U.S. coins. It starts with the story behind how the coin came to be, and it continues with the production of the coin itself over the years. Several coinage milestones are included in the series.

### Tribute to a slain president

Artists at the U.S. Mint started working on the Kennedy half dollar design even before a law authorizing the coin was passed.

President John F. Kennedy was assassinated on Nov. 22, 1963. Discussions about honoring Kennedy

President John F. Kennedy.

on a coin started within days of his death. So Mint artists started working on the design, too.

The quarter, half dollar, and dollar coins were all considered before the half dollar was chosen. The president's widow, Jacqueline Kennedy, did not want her late husband's image to replace George Washington on the quarter.

The Kennedy half dollar would replace the Franklin half dollar, which was first issued in 1948 to honor Benjamin Franklin.

President Lyndon B. Johnson signed the bill authorizing the Kennedy half dollar on Dec. 30, 1963. That allowed the Mint to start producing the coin right away in 1964.

### The silver 1964 Kennedy half dollars

The Mint started producing Kennedy half dollars in early 1964. The coins honoring the slain president became popular quickly. Many people wanted them. Because of that, the Mint produced many more Kennedy half dollars than expected – millions more, in fact.

In 1964, dimes, quarters, and half dollars were still composed mostly of silver. So 1964 Kennedy half dollars were

Obverse and reverse of 1964 Kennedy half dollar.

composed mostly of silver. This is the only year Kennedy half dollars were produced in the mostly silver composition.

### 1965-1969 Kennedy half dollars – still some silver

In 1965, the Mint started producing dimes and quarters in a mostly copper composition. The coins no longer contained silver.

The amount of silver in the Kennedy half dollar was reduced, but it still contained some silver. The Mint continued to use this composition for Kennedy half dollars through 1969.

No Kennedy half dollars were struck for circulation in 1970. Some 1970 Kennedy half dollars were produced, but they were available only in special collector sets sold by the Mint.

Obverse and reverse of 1965 Kennedy half dollar.

### The switch to clad

In 1971, the Mint started producing Kennedy half dollars in the mostly copper composition used for the dimes and quarters. It consists of a pure copper core with a nickel cladding over the top.

This same composition is used for Kennedy half dollars today.

### Put them all together

Thus, the Kennedy half dollar has seen three composition changes in its lifetime:

1. The traditional silver composition (1964) originally used for dimes, quarters, and half dollars
2. The reduced-silver composition (1965-1970)
3. The clad composition (1971-present)

### Celebrating the nation's birthday

The Kennedy half dollar was also part of another coinage milestone. The U.S. Mint issued special quarters, half dollars, and dollar coins to celebrate the nation's 200th birthday, or bicentennial, in 1976. The Mint started producing the coins after July 4, 1975, and continued to produce them through 1976.

The obverses of the coins stayed the same – George Washington on the quarter, John Kennedy on the half dollar, and former President Dwight

Obverse and reverse
of Bicentennial quarter.

Obverse and reverse of Bicentennial half dollar.

Obverse and
reverse of
Bicentennial
dollar.

D. Eisenhower on the dollar. But the dates on all of the coins read "1776-1976."

The reverses on each of the coins were changed. The quarter depicted a drummer boy from the Revolutionary War era. The half dollar depicted Independence Hall in Philadelphia, Pa.

And the dollar depicted the Liberty Bell with the moon behind it. This design honored the nation's space explorations and moon landings.

In 1977, the coins went back to their regular designs.

## How to collect them

**1964 Kennedy half dollars.** Many people saved 1964 Kennedy half dollars instead of spending them. They did this for a couple of reasons: the coins were popular mementoes of President Kennedy, and they were valued for their silver content after the composition of dimes and quarters was changed in 1965.

Because of this, few 1964 Kennedy half dollars can be found in circulation today. But some may still be out there. So be sure to check the date on any Kennedy half dollar you come across.

They can also be purchased from coin dealers. They aren't expensive, but rising prices for silver have driven up prices for silver Kennedy half dollars.

Obverse and reverse of 1964 Kennedy half dollar.

**1965-1969 Kennedy half dollars.** Many people hoarded Kennedy half dollars of 1965-1969 too. They were still valued for their silver content, even though they don't contain as much silver as the 1964 half dollars.

Because of this, few 1965-1969 Kennedy half dollars can be found in circulation. But you're more likely to find a 1965-1969 Kennedy half dollar than you are a 1964 Kennedy half dollar. Many people don't know that 1965-1969 Kennedy half dollars still contain some silver.

Kennedy half dollars of 1965-1969 also can be purchased from coin dealers. They don't cost as much as the 1964 half dollars, but rising silver prices still affect their cost.

**1971-present Kennedy half dollars.** When was the last time you or somebody you know got a Kennedy half dollar in change at a store? It's probably been quite a while, if ever.

Kennedy half dollars are big and bulky. Because of that, most people don't like to carry them around, and stores don't like to keep them in their cash registers. So you won't find many half dollars by searching pocket change.

Most banks, however, still stock rolls of half dollars. A roll of half dollars costs $10. Searching rolls is the best way to collect half dollars from circulation.

Kennedy half dollars dated 1971 and later also can be found in dealers'

## WHERE'S THE MINTMARK?

Kennedy half dollars with no mintmark were struck at the Philadelphia Mint. A "P" mintmark began  Mint mark 1964 appearing on half dollars produced at the Philadelphia Mint in 1980.

The Denver Mint also has produced Kennedy half dollars since the first issues of 1964. Half dollars produced at Denver have a "D" mintmark.

On 1964 Kennedy half dollars, the mintmark is located on the reverse below the eagle's right claw. Starting in 1968 and continuing today, the mintmark on half dollars can be found on the obverse between Kennedy's neck and the date.

bargain bins at coin shows and coin shops. Because they don't contain any silver, they don't cost as much as the earlier dates (1969 and earlier).

**Bicentennial half dollars.** The Bicentennial quarters and half dollars were once common in pocket change. But the older they get, the rarer it is to find one in pocket change.

Thus, rolls are the best way to find Bicentennial half dollars. There's a good chance of finding at least one example in any roll of half dollars.

Obverse and reverse of 1962 Franklin half dollar, replaced by the Kennedy half dollar in 1964.

# CHAPTER

## 10

# DOLLAR COINS– SOME LOVE THEM, SOME DON'T.

Obverse and reverse of
1979 Anthony dollar.

Dollars are some of the most popular U.S. coins. They're also some of the most unpopular.

How can that be? Here's how:

When people think of coin collecting, many think of big, shiny silver dollars from the 1800s and early 1900s. Old silver dollars are among the most popularly collected coins. If you go to a coin show or coin shop, you'll see rows of them lined up in dealers' cases.

Collectors like them because they have classic designs, they're big, and they have a nice, hefty feel when you hold one.

But as pocket change, dollar coins have never been popular. Why? Because they're big and have a hefty feel. Even the old silver dollars were not used much when they were new. A handful of them was a lot of weight in your pocket.

### The dollar coin goes on a diet

From the U.S. government's point of view, dollar coins make sense. A dollar coin costs more to produce than a paper dollar bill does, but the coin lasts longer. So it saves money in the long run.

But people have always liked carrying thin and light dollar bills better than carrying big and bulky dollar coins.

The government tried to change that when it introduced the Anthony dollar coin in 1979. The coin honored Susan B. Anthony, who lived from 1820 to 1906. She was active in promoting women's rights in the 1800s.

The Anthony dollar was much smaller and lighter than the old dollar coins. But it was almost the same size as a quarter. Because of that, the two were often confused. People sometimes spent the dollar coin while thinking they were spending a quarter.

The Anthony dollar didn't last long. It was struck only in 1979, 1980, and 1999.

### Try, try again

But, from the U.S. government's point of view, dollar coins make sense. So it tried again.

Obverse and reverse of 2002 Sacagawea dollar.

In 2000, the Sacagawea dollar coin was introduced. It depicts Sacagawea on the obverse. She was a young Native American woman who went with Lewis and Clark on their exploration of the American West. She gave birth to a son on the way, and on the coin, Sacagawea is shown carrying her son on her back.

The new dollar coin tried to correct the problems with the old Anthony dollar. It's still about the same size as the Anthony dollar, but several important changes were made:

- The Sacagawea dollar has a golden color. That helps it stand out in a handful of silver-colored nickels, dimes, and quarters.
- The Sacagawea dollar has a smooth edge instead of the rough, reeded edge on a quarter.

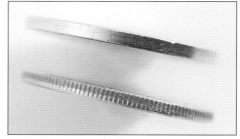

A smooth edge (top) and a reeded edge.

- The Sacagawea dollar has a wider border around its obverse and reverse designs. This, along with the smooth edge, helps people distinguish the coin from a quarter just by touch.

### And more designs, too

Starting in 2009, the U.S. Mint started changing the reverse of the Sacagawea dollar every year. The designs will honor the contributions of Native American tribes and individual Native Americans to the country's develop-

2009: Spread of Three Sisters reverse.

2010: Great Tree of Peace reverse.

2011: Wampanoag Treaty reverse.

ment and history.

Here are the designs that were issued for the first three years:

### 2009: Spread of Three Sisters.

The design honors the tradition and importance of agriculture in Native American culture.

### 2010: Great Tree of Peace.

This adorned belt symbolizes the Native American tribes that made

# PICK A THEME

Remember what we said early in this book: A coin collection can be anything you want it to be. Many people build a collection around on a theme. Examples include coins that depict ships or animals, or honor a certain event.

Here's an idea for a theme collection: coins related to the Lewis and Clark explorations. This collection could include the following coins:

- The Westward Journey nickels (see Chapter 6).

- A Sacagawea dollar.

- State quarters from the future states through which Lewis and Clark traveled.

- The Presidential dollar depicting Thomas Jefferson.

Theme collecting is limited only to your imagination and interests. After all, a coin collection can be whatever you want it to be.

Obverse and reverse of 1894 silver dollar.

# THEY'RE NOT SILVER ANYMORE

Some people call any dollar coin a "silver dollar," but the last U.S. dollar coin to actually contain silver was produced in 1935. Today's dollar coins are composed mostly of copper.

The term "silver dollar" should be used only for the old silver dollars, which actually contain silver.

# TWO FOR GROVER CLEVELAND

Grover Cleveland is the only U.S. president to serve two non-consecutive terms. In other words, his two terms did not come one after the other.

Cleveland served his first term from 1885 to 1889. Then Benjamin Harrison served from 1889 to 1893. Cleveland then served again from 1893 to 1897.

As a result, Cleveland is scheduled to be honored on two separate Presidential dollars in 2012.

President Grover Cleveland.

up the Iroquois Confederacy. The central figure on the belt, a great white pine, symbolizes the Onondaga Nation. The four squares around it represent the Mohawk, Oneida, Cayuga, and Seneca nations.

## 2011: Wampanoag Treaty.

This design honors the first treaty between Native Americans and European settlers, in 1621. It shows a European hand offering a peace pipe to a Native American hand.

### Honoring the presidents

In 2007, the U.S. Mint introduced a whole new series of dollar coins. This new series honors U.S. presidents. They are being produced in addition to the Native American dollars.

Four presidents will be honored in each year through 2015 in the order in which they served. Following is the schedule:

Common obverse for Presidential dollars.

**2007**
George Washington
John Adams
Thomas Jefferson
James Madison

**2008**
James Monroe
John Quincy Adams
Andrew Jackson
Martin Van Buren

**2009**
William Henry Harrison
John Tyler
James K. Polk
Zachary Taylor

**2010**
Millard Fillmore
Franklin Pierce

James Buchanan
Abraham Lincoln

**2011**
Andrew Johnson
Ulysses S. Grant
Rutherford B. Hayes
James A. Garfield

**2012**
Chester A. Arthur
Grover Cleveland
Benjamin Harrison
Grover Cleveland

**2013**
William McKinley
Theodore Roosevelt
William Howard Taft
Woodrow Wilson

**2014**
Warren Harding
Calvin Coolidge
Herbert Hoover
Franklin D. Roosevelt

**2015**
Harry S. Truman
Dwight D. Eisenhower
John F. Kennedy
Lyndon B. Johnson

**2016**
Richard M. Nixon
Gerald Ford

### Where to find them

Unfortunately, despite all the changes, dollar coins still aren't popular as pocket change. So the chances of finding Native American dollars and Presidential dollars in pocket change are small.

But local banks should have rolls of dollar coins. A roll costs $25.

Also, check the bargain bins at coin shows and shops.

# Presidential Dollar Coins
### 2007-2011 DOLLARS PICTURED

2007: George Washington

2007: John Adams

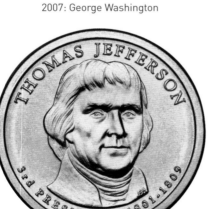

2007: Thomas Jefferson

2007: James Madison

# Presidential Dollar Coins
## 2007-2011 DOLLARS PICTURED

2008: James Monroe

2008: John Quincy Adams

2008: Andrew Jackson

2008: Martin Van Buren

2009: William Henry Harrison

2009: John Tyler

# PRESIDENTIAL DOLLAR COINS
## 2007-2011 DOLLARS PICTURED

2009: James K. Polk

2009: Zachary Taylor

2010: Millard Fillmore

2010: Franklin Pierce

2010: James Buchanan

2010: Abraham Lincoln

# Presidential Dollar Coins

2007–2011 DOLLARS PICTURED

2011: Andrew Johnson

2011: Ulysses S. Grant

2011: Rutherford B. Hayes

2011: James A. Garfield

# CHAPTER

## 11

# WELCOME TO THE COIN COLLECTING COMMUNITY.

Coin collecting isn't just a hobby. It's a community, too. You can pursue the hobby on your own if you want to. Many people, however, like to join in with others who share their interests. Coin collecting offers plenty of opportunities to do that.

**From 1799 until 1873, the U.S. Mint was an independent agency reporting to the president.**

## Coin clubs

Many cities and towns have local coin clubs. Their members meet regularly – usually monthly – to share their interests and learn from each other. Check the community events listings in your local newspaper for information on meeting times and place.

At the local meeting, you can also learn about state and regional organizations for coin collectors.

**The first Mint building was also the first Federal building constructed under the Constitution by the U.S. government.**

ANA headquarters.

## American Numismatic Association

The American Numismatic Association, founded in 1891, is the nation's largest organization for coin collectors. "Numismatics" (pronounced "new-miss-MAT-iks) is the collecting and studying of coins, paper money, tokens, medals, and similar items.

The ANA's headquarters are in Colorado Springs, Colo. They house a first-class museum, the Edward C. Rochette Money Museum, which is open to the public.

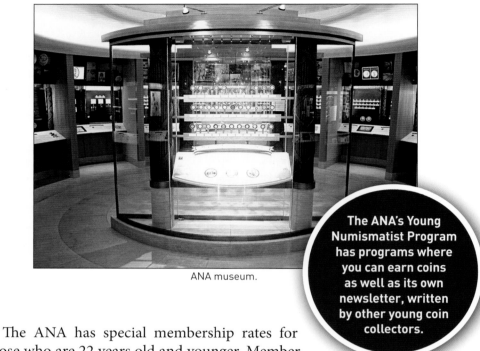

ANA museum.

The ANA's Young Numismatist Program has programs where you can earn coins as well as its own newsletter, written by other young coin collectors.

The ANA has special membership rates for those who are 22 years old and younger. Membership includes a subscription to the association's official magazine, *The Numismatist*.

To learn more about the ANA, see its website at www.money.org.

## Coin shows

Many local, state, and regional organizations sponsor coin shows. Some are just one day events at a local hall. The larger ones run several days. The American Numismatic Association sponsors two shows each year, which are among the largest in the country.

At shows, dealers offer collectible coins for sale. You can shop the offerings of many dealers in one spot. There might be 15 to 20 dealers at a smaller show. There can be several hundred dealers at a larger show.

The U.S. Mint and mints from other countries also have booths and displays at the larger shows.

Even if you don't buy anything, shows offer a great chance to look at a lot of coins.

The larger shows also have exhibits and seminars. Both are great opportunities to learn more about coins.

Many shows are free to attend. Some may have a small admission fee.

St. Eligius, a French metal worker from the 7th century, is considered the patron saint for coin collectors.

## Books

There are many more books on coin collecting. Some specialize in certain types of coin collecting, such as world coins. Many list values for coins.

Books on coin collecting can help you learn more about the hobby. They will help you make smart decisions when you start buying collectible coins from dealers or other collectors.

To learn more about coin-collecting books, see www.shopnumismaster.com.

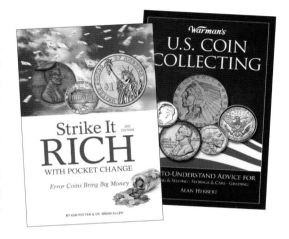

## Magazines

Magazines can also help you learn more about coin collecting. One of the best for new collectors is *Coins* magazine. A new issue comes out every month. It contains news on current happenings in the hobby and features that can help you learn more about specific coins

and the stories behind them.

It also lists upcoming coin shows big and small in all parts of the country. And each issue has a guide to current coin values.

To learn more about *Coins* magazine, see www.coinsmagazine.net.

### U.S. Mint

The U.S. Mint's website (www.usmint.gov) is also a good source of information for collectors. It has historical information on coins, and it also has information on new issues of coins.

Collectors can also buy new coins directly from the Mint through its website. Here are some of the coins that are available:

> The U.S. Mint also has a site for young collectors. Go to www.usmint. gov/kids/ to find out more.

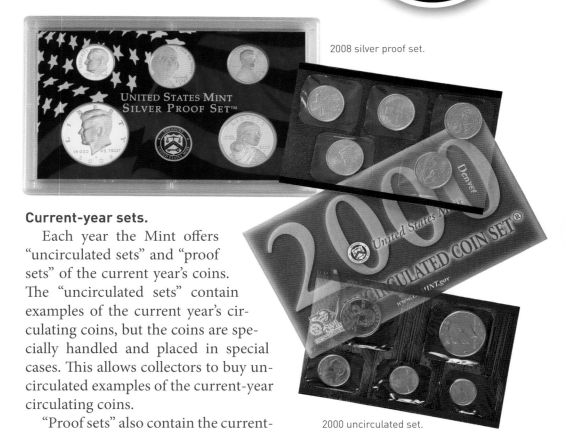

2008 silver proof set.

### Current-year sets.

Each year the Mint offers "uncirculated sets" and "proof sets" of the current year's coins. The "uncirculated sets" contain examples of the current year's circulating coins, but the coins are specially handled and placed in special cases. This allows collectors to buy uncirculated examples of the current-year circulating coins.

"Proof sets" also contain the current-

2000 uncirculated set.

year examples of circulating coins, but proof coins receive multiple strikings from the coining press. And the dies used to strike the coins are specially prepared. As a result, proof coins have mirrorlike surfaces and especially sharp design detail.

Commemorative coins are also still legal tender, meaning they can be used to pay for things.

1992 Columbus half dollar.

Capitol bicentennial silver dollar.

Jackie Robinson gold $5.

## Commemoratives.

Commemoratives are special coins that honor an event or person. They are authorized by specific laws and are official U.S. coins, but they are not intended to circulate.

The United States produced commemorative coins from 1892 through 1954. It started producing commemorative coins again in 1982.

Current-year commemoratives can be purchased through the Mint's website.

# START YOUR HUNT FOR
## NATIONAL TREASURE

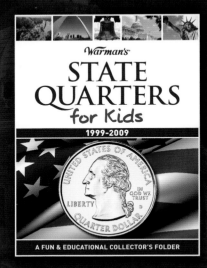

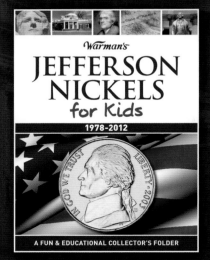

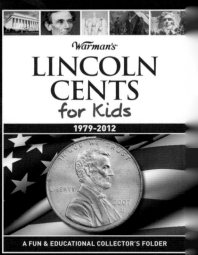

These and other great **Krause Publications** products are available at your local coin dealer, national bookseller or online store.